Women Coming Out of Exodus

40 - Day Devotional

Connie Freeman

CONTENTS

DEDICATION

First of all I would like to give thanks to God, my Lord and Savior Jesus Christ and the Holy Spirit who brought me out of my Exodus. My Exodus consisted of insecurities, depression, and low self-esteem. During the process He gave me the one scripture that I needed to stand on during my journey.

Philippians 4:13 (KJV) *"I can do all things through Christ who strengthens me."*

I would like to dedicate this book to my amazing husband, Vernon Freeman. You have been such a blessing to me. You have always encouraged, supported, and pushed me to be all that God has called me to be. I would also like to dedicate this book to my very special gifts from the Lord; my son Terrance, my daughter Tawoya, my daughter Toniah, my grandchildren, and my family. May God continue to bless you, prosper you, and protect you.

ACKNOWLEDGEMENT

I would like to acknowledge all those that have been a part of my life down through the years for your love, prayers, encouraging words, impartations, and support in every way collectively, and individually.

Thank you all for believing in the vision that the Lord is allowing me to birth and bring forth to maturity.

SPECIAL THANKS

I would like to give special thanks to Gretchel Dixon for her encouragement, giftings, and time she spent to make my dream a reality. May the Lord continue to bless you and your business (JaBrolka Publishing).

FORWARD

I am honored to share with you concerning the author, Mrs. Connie Freeman. She is an amazing Godly woman whom I have known for over 25 years. I met Connie while she was working in a beauty salon during my first year of college. I remember challenging her to perform different hairstyles. Amazingly, I have seen her grow personally, spiritually, and academically. She is a successful business owner of her own salon where she employs other hairstylists and now, I am witnessing her as an author of her first devotional book, I am Godly proud. Connie is a true friend and a Sister in Christ who I was honored to witness her birth "Coming Out of Exodus - Patio Talk" with Connie. It is amazing to hear her share the Word of God at her business, on social media, and in her back yard on the patio. God has truly blessed Connie with a large support system: her wonderful husband (Vernon), her beautiful children, her loving grandchildren, and her siblings. She truly has a powerful village. Connie is a true light in this new age whose assignment is to encourage women to succeed against any obstacle thrown in life. Connie has helped me, supported my family, and supported my ministry over the years. One scripture that accurately describes my sister Connie is,

Matthew 5:14-16ESV "You are the light of the world. A city set on a hill cannot be hidden. Nor do people light a lamp and put it under a basket, but on a stand, and it gives light to all in the house. In the same way, let your light shine

before others, so that they may see your good works and give glory to your Father who is in heaven." Amen.

I compel each of you to spend time in this devotional in an effort to come out of your own Exodus experiences. God Bless you and keep you is my prayer.

Reverend Rachel L. Hawkins-Luckett, Pastor

Allen Chapel A.M.E. Church, Atkins Arkansas 12th Episcopal District

DAY 1

John 14:3

Do not let your heart be troubled. Trust in God. Trust also in me.

Inspiration of today:

Women of Exodus – Our heart becomes troubled when we allow our trust to bounce around everywhere. Our heart bounces from our husband to our kids, to our workplace, and to our friends. When it comes back to us, we are confused and broken down. We have to learn to put our trust in God. The Lord will rebuild us and remove any trouble that is in our heart.

Reflection_____

_____

_____

_____

_____

_____

_____

_____

_____

_____

_____

_____

DAY 2

Jeremiah 33:6

Nevertheless, I will bring health and healing to it; I will heal my people and will let them enjoy abundant peace and security.

Inspiration of today:

Women of Exodus - When your house(body) is damaged, and your structure is falling down from depression, worries and insecurities stand on the Word of God. God said nevertheless I will bring health and healing to your house. He will rebuild the structure of your house with peace and joy.

Reflection_____

_____

_____

_____

_____

_____

_____

_____

_____

_____

_____

_____

_____

_____

_____

DAY 3

Psalm 23:4

Even though I walk through the valley of the shadow of death, I will fear no evil, for you are with me; your rod and your staff they comfort me.

Inspiration of today:

Women of Exodus – Even while you are wandering in your valley with the shadow of death surrounding you, just remember God's son Jesus Christ is guiding you with his rod. He also uses the Holy Spirit to comfort you and to keep you on the right path.

Reflection_____

_____

_____

_____

_____

_____

_____

_____

_____

_____

_____

_____

_____

_____

_____

CONNIE FREEMAN

DAY 4

Psalm 40: 1-2

I waited patiently for the Lord; and he inclined to me and heard my cry. He also brought me up out of a horrible pit, out of the miry clay and set my feet upon a rock and established my steps.

Inspiration of today:

Women of Exodus - Sometimes your pit is so deep that you can't find your way out. The darkness may overpower the light. Just remember that it does not matter how deep your pit is or how dark it is, when God hears your cry, he sends in his rescue worker(Jesus) and his equipment(the word) to pull you right out.

Reflection_____

_____

_____

_____

_____

_____

_____

_____

_____

_____

_____

_____

_____

DAY 5

Proverbs 18:21

Death and life are in the power of the tongue and they that love it shall eat the fruit there of.

Inspiration of today:

Women of Exodus - Sometimes the jail(pain) we are put in and the hospitals(sickness) we are laying in is keeping us connected to God's faith. So do not be quick to give up. Just speak God's word over your life and watch it start to work everything out.

Reflection_____

_____

_____

_____

_____

_____

_____

_____

_____

_____

_____

_____

_____

_____

DAY 6

Philippians 4:13

I can do all things through Christ who strengthens me.

Inspiration of today:

Women of Exodus - Even when we are coming to or going through our darkest valleys, remember when our strength is weak, with God's strength we can conquer anything.

Reflection_____

_____

_____

_____

_____

_____

_____

_____

_____

_____

_____

_____

_____

_____

_____

_____

_____

DAY 7

Luke 13:11-13

And behold, there was a women which had a spirit of infirmity eighteen years, and was bowed together, and could in no wise lift up herself. And when Jesus saw her, he called her to him, and said unto her, Woman, thou art loosed from thine infirmity. And he laid his hands on her: and immediately she was made straight, and glorified God.

Inspiration of today:

Women of Exodus - It does not matter what problem you have or how long you have had them. Jesus can put a plug in those problems that are draining you dry.

Reflection_____

_____

_____

_____

_____

_____

_____

_____

_____

_____

_____

DAY 8

Proverb 3:5-6

Trust in the Lord with all your heart and lead not to your own understanding in all your ways acknowledge him and he will direct your path.

Inspiration of today:

Women of Exodus - There are times when we try to fix the path that we are on ourselves. It is during those times that we begin to get overwhelmed. Stop what you are doing and trust God. The path you are on will become straight.

Reflection_____

_____
_____
_____
_____
_____
_____
_____
_____
_____
_____
_____
_____
_____
_____

DAY 9

- -

Luke 6:38

Give and it will be given to you. A good measure pressed down shaken together and running over will be poured into your lap. For with the measure you use it will be measured to you.

Inspiration of today:

Women of Exodus - We are givers. We give our love, time, money, and our hearts. Sometimes it seems like we are all emptied out, but just remember God is measuring what you are using. He will pour it all back into you.

Reflection_____

_____

_____

_____

_____

_____

_____

_____

_____

_____

_____

_____

_____

_____

_____

_____

DAY 10

Mark 10:52

Jesus said go your faith has healed you. At once he was able to see, and he began to follow Jesus on the way.

Inspiration of today:

Women of Exodus - Some of your bondage has enslaved you and became your master of darkness. Jesus will call out to you who are spiritually blind and give you sight.

Reflection_____

_____

_____

_____

_____

_____

_____

_____

_____

_____

_____

_____

_____

_____

_____

_____

_____

_____

DAY 11

James 1:2-4

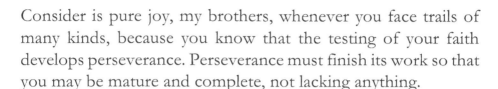

Consider is pure joy, my brothers, whenever you face trails of many kinds, because you know that the testing of your faith develops perseverance. Perseverance must finish its work so that you may be mature and complete, not lacking anything.

Inspiration of today:

Women of Exodus - When trouble falls on you, just know that God allows these troubles in our lives as a test to demonstrate our belief; that the testing of faith produces patience. So do not be in a rush, wait on God and pass your test.

Reflection_____

_____
_____
_____
_____
_____
_____
_____
_____
_____
_____
_____
_____
_____

DAY 12

Psalm 94:19

When anxiety was great within me, your consolation brought joy to my soul.

Inspiration of today:

Women of Exodus – Regardless of how dark it gets in your house(body) just remember, God's comforter(the Holy Spirit) will bring joy to your soul if you let him.

Reflection_____

_____

_____

_____

_____

_____

_____

_____

_____

_____

_____

_____

_____

_____

_____

_____

_____

DAY 13

Deuteronomy 31:8

The lord himself goes before you and will be with you. He will never leave nor forsake you. Do not be afraid; do not be discouraged.

Inspiration of today:

Women of Exodus - While traveling through those dark journeys of anxiety, depression, and insecurity, remember the Lord is taking those trips with you and just like a vacation He will give you peace and rest at the end.

Reflection_____

_____

_____

_____

_____

_____

_____

_____

_____

_____

_____

_____

_____

_____

_____

_____

DAY 14

- -

John 5:8

Jesus saith unto him, get up, pick up your mat and walk.

Inspiration of today:

Women of Exodus - Your mat that you have been laying on is worn out. It has so many wounds from your past disappointments and hurt. God said get up, pick up your wounded mat and go into your healing.

Reflection_____

_____

_____

_____

_____

_____

_____

_____

_____

_____

_____

_____

_____

_____

_____

_____

_____

DAY 15

John 11:43-44

Now when he had said these things, He cried with a loud voice Lazarus, come forth and he who died came out bound hand and foot with graveclothes, and his face was wrapped with a cloth. Jesus said to them, Loose him and let him go.

Inspiration of today:

Women of Exodus - When Jesus raised you out of bondage, He stripped the graveclothes of depression, unforgiveness, and insecurities that are holding you down. He will wrap you with his grace and mercy.

Reflection_____

_____

_____

_____

_____

_____

_____

_____

_____

_____

_____

_____

_____

_____

DAY 16

Psalm 51:10

Create in me a clean heart O God and renew a steadfast spirit within me.

Inspiration of today:

Women of Exodus - As you walk in flesh on this earth, trash is getting dumped in your heart every day. Different spirits are loitering around in your house(body) which leaves you drained and weak. Even when your house(body) seems so dirty, God gives you cleaning instructions(his word) to use to clean the trash from your heart and remove the wrong spirits within your soul.

Reflection_____

_____

_____

_____

_____

_____

_____

_____

_____

_____

_____

_____

_____

DAY 17

Job 1:8

Then the Lord said to Satan, Have you considered my servant Job? There is no one on earth like him, he is blameless and an upright man who fears God and shuns evil.

Inspiration of today:

Women of Exodus - Sometimes you have been considered just like Job in order to see were your faith in God stands. So, do not let the challenges you are facing keep you from trusting what God has for you. Keep the Faith and watch him work.

Reflection_____

_____

_____

_____

_____

_____

_____

_____

_____

_____

_____

_____

_____

_____

_____

_____

DAY 18

Psalms 126:5-6

Those who sow with tears will reap with songs of joy. Those who go out weeping carrying seed to sow, will return song of joy carrying sheaves with them.

Inspiration of today:

Women of Exodus - You may shed a lot of tears traveling throughout this journey of pain. Just know that Jesus takes each one of your tear drops and He is watering your garden of joy.

Reflection_____

_____

_____

_____

_____

_____

_____

_____

_____

_____

_____

_____

_____

_____

_____

_____

_____

DAY 19

James 4:7

Submit yourselves then to God. Resist the devil and he will flee from you.

Inspiration of today:

Women of Exodus - There may be times when your bondage gets so heavy that you cannot see your way out. When you give God the authorization to have surgery on your mind, body, and soul it will restrain the power of Satan spirits over you. Then you will be recovering under the Holy Spirit care.

Reflection_____

_____

_____

_____

_____

_____

_____

_____

_____

_____

_____

_____

_____

_____

_____

_____

DAY 20

- -

Psalm 127:1

Useless the Lord, Build the house, They labor in vain who build it; unless the Lord guard the city, The watch stay awake in vain.

Inspiration of today:

Women of Exodus - Stop trying to build your own house(soul) with your man-made material. You are using the wrong material. Unless the Lord builds your house all your work will be in vain.

Reflection_____

_____

_____

_____

_____

_____

_____

_____

_____

_____

_____

_____

_____

_____

_____

_____

_____

_____

_____

DAY 21

Matthew 11:28

Come to me all you who are weary and burdened, and I will give you rest.

Inspiration of today:

Women of Exodus - The worries and sin of this world will change the structure of your house(body). You are no longer sleeping at night because you are carrying so many burdens. Now your house is leaning. God knew these days would come and He has the best contractor that you can call to get your structure lined up with your foundation. His name is Jesus Christ, and He will give you rest.

Reflection_____

_____

_____

_____

_____

_____

_____

_____

_____

_____

_____

_____

_____

DAY 22

Psalm 27:10

Though my father and mother forsake me, the Lord will receive me.

Inspiration of today:

Women of Exodus - You may have been physically or emotionally abandoned in your life by people that you trusted and loved. The rejection broke you down physically, mentally, and spiritually. Satan makes you think that you have been declined but the Lord has already received you.

Reflection_____

_____

_____

_____

_____

_____

_____

_____

_____

_____

_____

_____

_____

_____

_____

_____

DAY 23

Jeremiah 29:11

For I know the plans I have for you, declares the Lord, plans for peace and not for evil to give you a future and a hope.

Inspiration of today:

Women of Exodus - The situation of the world today has detoured your plan that God had for you. It has taken you on a road of depression, insecurities, low self-esteem, and unforgiveness. God said this road I have for you is a plan of peace and not evil. A future of good hope.

Reflection_____

_____

_____

_____

_____

_____

_____

_____

_____

_____

_____

_____

_____

DAY 24

- -

John 16:33

I have told you these things so that in me you may have peace. In this world you will have trouble but take heart; I have overcome the world.

Inspiration of today:

Women of Exodus - This world of trouble has turned you upside down. Your rest and peace have been replaced with sleepless nights and worrying days. Just know that your life does not have to stay that way. You can have peace in the Lord because He has already overcame this world.

Reflection_____

_____

_____

_____

_____

_____

_____

_____

_____

_____

_____

_____

_____

_____

DAY 25

Luke 8:43-44

And a woman having an issue of blood of twelve years, which had spent all her living upon physicians neither could be healed of any. She came up behind him and touched the edge of his garment and immediately her issue stop.

Inspiration of today:

Women of Exodus - Today you might feel that there is no way out with the issue that you are facing now. Jesus said just believe and your faith has already healed your issue.

Reflection_____

_____
_____
_____
_____
_____
_____
_____
_____
_____
_____
_____
_____
_____
_____
_____

DAY 26

Psalm 34:17-18

The righteous cry out and the Lord heard them, he delivers them from all their troubles. The Lord is close to the brokenhearted and saves those who are crushed in spirit.

Inspiration of today:

Women of Exodus - One of the worst feelings in the world is to experience hurt and feel that you do not have anyone around to help. You have cried out many nights from the pain of the bondage that you are carrying around. Remember God hears your cry, and He will deliver you from all your troubles.

Reflection_____

_____
_____
_____
_____
_____
_____
_____
_____
_____
_____
_____
_____
_____
_____

DAY 27

Peter 5:7

Cast all your anxiety on him because he cares for you.

Inspiration of today:

Women of Exodus – Women have a lot of baggage to deal with on a daily basis. There are times that women get so stressed, and they can do it without even trying. It is a promise that all you have to do is believe God. He will receive all your worries and carry them for you.

Reflection_____

_____

_____

_____

_____

_____

_____

_____

_____

_____

_____

_____

_____

_____

_____

_____

_____

DAY 28

Psalm 9:9

The lord also will be a refuge for the oppressed, a refuge in times of trouble.

Inspiration of today:

Women of Exodus - While you are walking in the valley of your storms. Know that the Lord is covering you with his shelter of protection.

Reflection_____

_____

_____

_____

_____

_____

_____

_____

_____

_____

_____

_____

_____

_____

_____

_____

_____

DAY 29

Joshua 1:9

This is my command- be strong and courageous. Do not be afraid or discouraged. For the Lord your God is with you wherever you go.

Inspiration of today:

Women of Exodus – Life can be full of challenges, pain, and tough decisions. Depression is waiting to come visit you, but remember the Lord commands you to be strong and courageous. Because He is with you wherever you go.

Reflection_____

_____

_____

_____

_____

_____

_____

_____

_____

_____

_____

_____

_____

_____

_____

_____

DAY 30

2Samuel 22:29

For thou art my lamp, O Lord and the Lord will lighten my darkness.

Inspiration of today:

Women of Exodus - The light in your lamp of peace might have become dark in the mist of storms. The Lord will give you his oil to light up your darkness so you can see your way through.

Reflection_____

_____

_____

_____

_____

_____

_____

_____

_____

_____

_____

_____

_____

_____

_____

_____

_____

_____

DAY 31

Roman 15:13

Now the God of hope fill you with all joy and peace in believing, that ye may abound in hope, through the power of the Holy Spirit.

Inspiration of today:

Women of Exodus – There are times when your hope is led by the wrong spirit. It will have you wanting something to happen that is far from becoming true. God will fill you with the power of the Holy Spirit and will restore your joy and peace.

Reflection_____

DAY 32

Psalm 34:4

I sought the Lord, and he heard me. And delivered me from all my fears.

Inspiration of today:

Women of Exodus - You may have unforgiveness in your heart from past hurt that is making you feel afraid and lost, but there is a man name Jesus who can deliver you from this. He can renew your mind and restore your heart.

Reflection_____

_____

_____

_____

_____

_____

_____

_____

_____

_____

_____

_____

_____

_____

_____

CONNIE FREEMAN

DAY 33

- -

2 Corinthians 12:9-10

"And he said to me, my grace is sufficient for you, for my power is perfect in weakness, therefore, I will boast all the more gladly about my weaknesses, so that Christ's power may rest on me."

Inspiration of today:

Women of Exodus - You may have several thorns of depression, anxiety, or loneliness that is attach to you. It does not matter how many you have, the Heavenly Father grace is sufficient for you and the power of Christ will began to purge those thorns.

Reflection_____

_____

_____

_____

_____

_____

_____

_____

_____

_____

_____

_____

_____

_____

_____

_____

_____

DAY 34

Job 33:30

To bring back his soul from the pit, to be enlightened with the light of the living.

Inspiration of today:

Women of Exodus - Satan has done a background check on you to see what he can use to keep you in that dark pit. The more he push that button the deeper it gets. There is nothing God cannot do. He can enlighten you with His light so you can see your way out.

Reflection_____

_____

_____

_____

_____

_____

_____

_____

_____

_____

_____

_____

_____

_____

_____

_____

_____

DAY 35

Matthew 6:34

So don't worry about tomorrow for tomorrow will bring its own worries. Today's trouble is enough for today.

Inspiration of today:

Women of Exodus – As you live day to day, the pain of life can cause you anxiety and mental destress. This can cause you to be concerned about how you are going to pay your bills or feed your family. God said the trouble of tomorrow has its own worries. If he feeds the bird, how much more important are you?

Reflection_____

_____
_____
_____
_____
_____
_____
_____
_____
_____
_____
_____
_____
_____
_____

DAY 36

— —

2Corintian 3:17

Now the Lord is the spirit and where the spirit of the Lord is there is freedom.

Inspiration of today:

Women of Exodus - The bondage of Spirits that have set-up camp in your house(body) have started a fire of depression and insecurities. The only way to put that fire out is with the Spirit of the Lord.

Reflection_____

_____

_____

_____

_____

_____

_____

_____

_____

_____

_____

_____

_____

_____

_____

_____

DAY 37

Romans 5:5

And hope does not put us to shame because Gods love has been poured out into our hearts through the Holy Spirit, Who has been given to us.

Inspiration of today:

Women of Exodus - Your heart may have been broken and the hope you had for your life has been stored in a place of darkness. The Holy Spirit has been poured into your heart to bring your hope to light.

Reflection_____

_____

_____

_____

_____

_____

_____

_____

_____

_____

_____

_____

_____

_____

_____

DAY 38

Ephesians 2:8-10

For by grace you have been saved through faith and this is not your own doing, it is the gift of God. Not a result of works, so that no one may boast. For we are His workmanship, created in Christ Jesus for good works, which God prepared beforehand, that we should walk in them.

Inspiration of today:

Women of Exodus - The feeling of worthlessness will start crippling you from living the gift of God's plan. It will have you feeling useless when you try to achieve goals and then fail. You are not a failure in Christ. For by grace you have been saved through faith.

Reflection_____

_____

_____

_____

_____

_____

_____

_____

_____

_____

_____

_____

DAY 39

Jeremiah 1:5

Before I formed you in the womb, I knew you and before you were born, I consecrated you, I appointed you a prophet to the nations.

Inspiration of today:

Women of Exodus - Were you ever asked what you wanted to be when you grow up? You may have been eager to answer that question not realizing that the world troubles and situations could change your whole life in minutes. Regardless of where you are today, good or bad remember, God knew you before you were born, and He made you with a purpose in mind.

Reflection_____

_____
_____
_____
_____
_____
_____
_____
_____
_____
_____
_____
_____

DAY 40

Mark 11:24

Therefore I say into you, what things so ever you deserve when you pray believe that you receive them, and you shall have them.

Inspiration of today:

Women of Exodus - When tribulation and hardships comes upon you, it may make you feel negative, or weak, and in your mind you feel that there is no connection. God says that there is connection through prayer if you believe. He says that if you have faith, you can receive, and you shall have them.

Reflection_____

_____

_____

_____

_____

_____

_____

_____

_____

_____

_____

_____

_____

PRAYER

Father God,

I come to you with my head bowed down and my arms open wide. Father God, I pray for the person reading this book. I pray that you release the bondage of the demonic spirits of depression, low self-esteem, insecurities, anger, jealousy, envy, abuse, loneliness, and feeling worthless. I decree and declare that this bondage has been released in Jesus name I pray...

Amen

Stay connected to Connie Freeman by:

Email her at: conniesno12@yahoo.com

Or

Connect with her on Social Media

Made in the USA
Columbia, SC
23 November 2022

71669957R00052